AFTERTHOUGHTS

AFTERTHOUGHTS

By

Victor M. Lee

ISBN 978-0-557-14061-9

TABLE OF CONTENTS

IN MEMORY OF:

This book is dedicated to the memory of:

My Pops:	John L. Lee (My Hero)
Grandmother:	Willie Mae Henton (Big Momma)
Grandfather:	Knute Henton (Daddy Knute)
Biological Grandfather:	Harper Sturgis
Aunt:	Augustine Akins
Aunt:	Viola Andrews

PREFACE

First of all I would like to thank my Lord and Savior Jesus Christ for providing me with a whole lot of grace and forgiveness. Psalm 27:1-"The Lord is my light and salvation—whom shall I fear? The Lord is the strength of my life—of whom shall I be afraid?"

Poetry is utilizing words as raw materials but instead of creating a product that you can physically touch or see. It is creating a picture, an idea or story in a meaningful pattern. Thus, you are creating a product that you can't physically touch but it touches you...emotionally, you can't see it with your eyes but you can visualize in your mind, and poetry has no limits or barriers. It invokes thoughts and powerful feelings in both listeners and readers.

Afterthoughts is an autobiography in which poetry is the chosen literary genre. Each poem is a depiction of love found, love lost, heartbreak, hardship, success, inspiration and much more that I have experienced in my lifetime.

About me...well I'm a country boy from Camden, Arkansas (population of about 11,000) and a proud graduate of Camden High School (Panthers). I am a Disabled U.S. Army Veteran who served in Saudi Arabia and Kuwait during Operation Desert Shield and Operation Desert Storm (Persian Gulf War). I am extremely honored and proud to have had the opportunity to serve in the Armed Forces of the greatest country in the world. I have a Masters Degree in Community Service from Michigan State University and a Masters Degree in Human Resources from Central Michigan University. **Not bad for an old "kuntry boy" from Camden.**

Thanks to my mother Barbara Porter the greatest mother in the world. Mom thank you so very much you have been there for me through thick and thin. Mom you have provided me with so much wisdom and wise counsel throughout the years. There is no doubt that I would not have made it this far without your love and support. I Love You Mom!

Special thanks to the "old Man"-Douglas Porter 1) for being a good husband to my mom 2) for being an exemplary male role model for me. If I can become half the man he is…I still will have achieved greatness. Shout out to my brothers and sisters: Tina, Tyrone, Felecia, Zemeka, Roxanne, Billie, Ashley, Douglass Jr., and Joshua. Yes, that means there are ten of us.

Thanks to my children they are the best children a dad could ever have: Chrystal (has a mouth like her father), Christopher (has an attitude like his father) and Charice (unfortunately she looks like her father). I would be remiss if I don't mention my granddaughter Mikayla.

Last but certainly not least is the love of my life my best friend, lover and soulmate: Gigi. Gigi is an abbreviation for Genuine Girl. Because she is the most genuine, loving and caring person I have ever known. It is said that behind every good man is a great woman. In my case it is a phenomenally awesome woman. See...she saved my life. Before I met her I wasn't living...I was just waiting to die. She has shown me what unconditional love is all about. She is my inspiration and motivation. Gigi...I Love You…ILYIAB ☺

My Hero

Nope...he was not the strongest—smartest—fastest

His biography is not filled with anything unique

He couldn't leap tall buildings with a single bound

The fact he survived in prison—his most identifiable feat

Abandoned us for another so very early in my life—far
too soon for me

Father? Yes...Daddy? No! There is a big difference
I think you agree

Love my father? Hell No! More like spite—contempt—hate

He was a sperm donor plain and simple...he was way too late

Give him a chance...why should I...after what he did

He left us to fin for ourselves—yes a wife and two small kids

Twenty five plus times the Earth has since circled the Sun

His time of incarceration has concluded it's done

My mom told me in order to continue life in order to truly live

My darling son read Luke 15:11 and learn how to forgive

Anxious—nervous—agitated—shaky best describes my mood

What do I say—how do I act around this dude

A fragile frail man of slight build—what a change...so many years

The feelings of hatred and pain...replaced with heart felt tears

We exchanged a loving hug and an everlasting embrace

Distant memories of a childhood without a Dad erased

Dad...yes I said it—a lifelong dream has finally come true

My kids have a Grandpa from whence they came they now knew

Considering our non-existent history—when it was all said and done

I would say we grew as close as any father and son

That Thirteenth Day of January in the year 2006

That fatal phone call came—one I will never forget

The Almighty said: "Your times up—my child we must go"

I not only lost my best friend…my dad—I also lost my HERO!

Stop the Violence

A 16 year old honor student killed walking home from school

A 20 year old college student killed at a dance that aint cool

My Brothers and sisters when are we going to learn?

All violence does is have someone's loved one
end up in an urn

Violence begets more violence that's a well known fact

We need to start thinking before we act

Life is not a video game and you hit reset and people
come back alive

Peace and harmony is the direction in which we need to strive

94% of blacks are killed by blacks not by our brethren
who are white

It takes a mature person to walk away instead of argue and fight

With statistics like this we are putting the Klan out of work

If you're disrespected THINK don't lose your cool and go berserk

THINK about the heartbreak it would cause your significant others

THINK about your mom…dad…wife…kids…sisters and brothers

Violence has never proved that anyone was better than you or me

The cemetery is full of people who just had to prove they were a G!

Don't Give Up...Try

Life is about what you do when you get knocked down

You need to pick yourself up…dust yourself off and
get up off the ground

Having a tough time with the person who is the answer
to your prayers

You quickly learn there are no elevators to love you have
to take the stairs

Divorce rate over 50%...today's tendency is to call
it quits and pack it in

Gain knowledge from my mistakes learn from where I've been

You might think the grass is greener on the other side of the fence

Stop thinking with the wrong head…use some common sense

Talk to her openly…before you think about creeping with another

She deserves that respect…considering…she is your
children's mother

It doesn't matter who's at fault or who's wrong or right

You're trying to save your marriage so don't give up
without a fight

Close your mouth and open your ears and listen to
what she has to say

God gave us twice as many ears as mouth so
he wanted us to listen…ok

Look deeply into her eyes and fall in love again
…after all she is your wife

No…it's not too late today is the first day of the rest of your life

A passionate long embrace as you hold each other and begin to cry

See the wonderful things that can happen when you try

Beauty, Brains, and Black

Beauty, Brains, and Black
I am proud and not ashamed to say…
These are the qualities I'm searching for today
A Nubian and modern day queen
Whose beauty is the likes that have never been seen
Yeah, I say proudly, Beauty, Brains, and Black
Beauty both inside and out
I heard that beauty is only skin deep but
Ugly goes clean to the bone
But true beauty goes beyond the bone and all the way to
The soul…yeah…the soul that can only be obtained from
Being the descendants of African Slaves and
Daughters of sharecroppers
Yeah, I say proudly, Beauty, Brains, and Black
The Courage of Harriett Tubman, the grace of Maya Angelou
The brains and Wisdom of Oprah…
Kudos Barbara Jordan, Shirley Chisholm, and YES! My MOM
For showing that black women have the brains
The intellect to achieve the unachievable and
attain the unattainable
Yeah, I say proudly, Beauty, Brains, and Black
I'm considered successful and have a few college degrees
But if you are not a sista step out of the way please

In order for me to be Pro-Black does not mean
I am anti-anything…it simply means that the woman
Who I share my hope, desires, future, and dreams
Must have the three B's
Beauty, Brains, and Black

Black is Beautiful

Soiled…stained with dirt—enveloped in darkness a black night
Lacking of hue—absent of brightness and light
Gloomy…pessimistic…dismal—a black outlook
Sullen…hostile…evil…wicked—dark as soot
Black market...Black Friday…black comedy…black mail
Characterizations that make me want to holler make me want to yell
Our ancestors who rode on the Amistad—only 38 survive
They bestowed the courage, strength, will, and ambition to thrive
Don't insult our intelligence by combining Ebony and Phonics
Brilliant people—who speak many dialects our language—not Ebonics
A dignified group of people with varying success and pedigree
Mandela—Oprah—Stevie just to name three
An extensive journey from matriarchs such as Aunt Jemima
To the must powerful man in the world…President Obama
Dr. King said it first and I proudly say it again
Judge us based on the content of our character and not the color of our skin
2009…scary—tense—stressful economic times a sign things are on track
Ironic—somewhat comical when businesses once again operate in the **BLACK!**

You Are...

You are…so very warm and sincere
You are…who I appreciate so dear
You are…my brilliant and bright star
You are…who I cherish because of who you are
You are…so awesome and amazing
You are…the woman I've been craving
You are…more exquisite than the finest work of art
You are…the keeper of the key to my heart
You are…who I am devoted and treasure
You are… who brings me joy and pleasure
You are…an angel from above
You are…the woman with whom I've fallen in love

Success

Achievement—triumph—the attainment of a goal
The true meaning of success can only be found deep in your soul
Some may define success with a car—house—money or even a job
For me: its sharing my life with the one who makes my heart throb
I look in the mirror and honestly I don't know what she sees
By her words and actions she is really in love with me
Love must be blind since we are the epitome of beauty and the beast
She is so charming—elegant—graceful to say the least
She loves me because of who I am and not my title
I'll put a ring on her finger and take her straight to David's Bridal☺
She loves me because of my character and not my position
This loving woman will stick with me no matter the condition
She loves me because she believes in me and what I stand for
She's the woman of my dreams and only one I love and adore
With an angel like this I know I have certainly been blessed
Now you know and understand why and how I define success

Make It Rain

Tonight I had a really good cry…in my own way I made it rain
I let it all out the emotion—fear—hurt and the pain
For the first time in a very long time I felt alone
No one in which I can depend as I sat at home
My feelings devastated…I am all torn up inside
Paralyzed by the overwhelming pain I just sat here and cried
I felt so very much abandoned like I didn't even matter
The more time I thought about it…I became even sadder
I felt like an afterthought…like I don't even rank
It is not my intention to be mean…just being frank
I truly don't ask for very much out of life…damn! What the heck!
All I ask…is to be treated with love dignity and respect
Love can be complex more importantly it's a word of action
All I'm asking for is quality time…not a whole lot
…just a small fraction
I'm not meant to be alone especially in times like this
No medicine can cure my affliction except her warm
embrace and kiss
I felt abandoned and so alone…it weighed heavy on my brain
The bottom line is I'm all cried out and in my own
way made it rain

Pleasure

The premonition of her instantly sends me to that place of fantasy
That region of my mind reserved for her and me
Ecstasy...elation best describes the mood in this place
Mission—to put an everlasting smile upon her face
Intentions are delectable and quite simple to measure
Goal—to give her mind and body erotic pleasure
Ever so softly my lips graze her back and the nape of her neck
Destination—"where no man has gone before" like Star Trek
Caressing her tenderly...gingerly...fondling inside her thigh
Her sounds of euphoria rang lustily throughout the night
I ventured south of her navel as I grabbed her hips
My objective—to open my mouth and moisten her lips
I drew her close and could hear our hearts beat as one
Our body's rhythmic gyrations had only just begun
Sultry, graceful movements—an in and out flow
She whispered gently—"that's it BIG DADDY nice and slow"
Erotic melodies heard...seismic eruptions can't be stopped
Clinched fist...stiff leg...Oh, Yeah! I've hit the G-Spot
She grasped my neck...she began to claw my back
The ultimate goal achieved...we were about to climax
I held her—looked deep into her eyes—a priceless treasure
Thanks' for a night filled with intimacy, passion, and the ultimate
PLEASURE!

Dead Man Walking

Time and time again things just don't turn out right
I did my best…I fought the good fight
Simple…"I want to love somebody and have them love me back"
No damn game playing and that's a fact!
This is for keeps—no doubt she had the key to my heart
I dreaded each and every moment we spent apart
For sure—treated her with dignity…tender, love, and care
Couldn't find another who loved her like me anywhere
One day it was this…and the next day it was that
Excuses—she would leave me hanging at the drop of a hat
Anticipating her companionship—craving for the sound of her voice
Deprived of her time and affection—I detached…I had no choice
Soul on empty—debilitated from grief—so much agony—too much pain
Harder than any physical affliction—cerebral and psychological drain
All cried out…too much heartache…too much hurt
Maybe it's not so bad six feet beneath the dirt
Dejected…Despair…Despondent…sick and tired of talking
Heartbreak is hell…emotionally I'm a Dead Man Walking

Displaced Emotions

Dear Heavenly Father…I sinned today
Without thinking I felt I had something important to say
In the process I was really upset—angry—mad
Like an idiot I said some things I should not had
I need to stop and think before I speak
Or I'm going to continue to find myself up shit creek
Prior to opening my mouth I need to engage my brain
To prevent me from saying something…when I should refrain
I was focused on me and didn't keep my eye on the prize
Look at me now…humbly having to apologize
To respond while infuriated makes absolutely no sense
On bended knee I humble myself and ask forgiveness
If the people I hurt don't want me back I understand
Acting with anger…I showed myself, less than a man
I hurt those most important to me the one's I truly love
I now look to you Lord for guidance from above
Help me control my tongue—my emotional outburst
I should have known you were going to direct me to a Bible verse
Adhere to the word and it will keep you out of trouble and danger
James 1:19…be quick to listen, slow to speak and slow to anger

It's Just Me

Raised in Camden down deep in Arkansas home state of Bill
Proud to be from the Dirty South…just keepin it real
You could smell the stench of the paper mill all over town
Red clay dirt and mosquitos so big they'd knock you down
Hot and humid summer days and football on Friday nights
Camden—Fairview football game what a scene an awesome sight
I guess we were poor—we didn't know either way
A hard working mom that provided for us each and every day
She worked at least two to three jobs all of the time
Waitressing and cleaning up people houses just to make a dime
Living in the projects paying sixty bucks a month for rent
We were taught to appreciate everything as heaven sent
When momma spoke we listened she didn't want to hear our voice
Church on Sunday—respect your elders…there was no choice
Hanging out smoking weed…that Acapulco Gold me and my crew
Drinking Thunderbird, Mad Dog and some Home Brew
Cruising up and down the street looking for some honey's to pull
A nice buzz…feeling good drinking that Schlitz Malt Liquor Bull
Jackpot! My Mack game is on and poppin tonight
Getting digits and pulling females left and right

Time to change—getting way too old for this same old shit

Time to mature from a boy to a man and come legit

Thank God the fruit does not fall far from the tree

All of my mom's life lessons began to come back to me

Do onto others as you would have them do onto you-
The Golden Rule

Christian values and beliefs—treat all people like a precious jewel

Place others needs before your own—a larger calling—the
greater good

Bear in mind it takes a village to raise a child—the entire hood

Pay it forward help others who can't help themselves
as simple as ABC

Uncomplicated—humble—plain and simple it's just me

Welcome To My World

The great blessings of life are within us all and within our grasp;
Instead we close our eyes, heart, and soul
And like people in the dark we stumble upon the very thing
We search for.....without finding it....
Always keep your heart open because that is the only way you will
Find love and love find you; love can't find a closed heart!
So open your heart and allow me to expand your horizons
Go ahead take it, yes a first class ticket to "My World"
If you are ready to make a leap of faith—I will be there to catch you
Welcome to my world a world of hope that runs eternal
A world in which the sun is always shining and the skies are always blue
My world is this way because unlike any other it revolves around you
You're the Sun to my Earth, comfort to my heart, stimulation to my soul
It's not difficult or complex; I'm not full of shit and just in it for sex
So, welcome to my world...a place with room only for you
Built to ensure that all your fantasies, desires and dreams come true
You will not find it on any map, globe, atlas, or chart
You already have the key to my world; yep, the key to my soul and heart

If You're Asking...

If you're asking if I need you...the answer is forever
If you're asking if I will leave you...the answer is never
If you're asking if I'm certain...the answer is real
If you're asking do I cherish you...the answer is I always will
If you're asking what I value...the answer is you
If you're asking if I love you...the answer is I do
If you're asking how true my love is...the answer is with all my heart
If you're asking will I be faithful...the answer is till death do us part
If you're asking do I trust you...the answer is with my life
If you're asking what's my dream...the answer is for you to be my wife

Straight From The Heart

Other ladies approached me…I didn't give them a single thought

It was a no brainer…because yours is the heart I sought

First we were friends and that was cool you helped build my self esteem

Then we discovered we're soulmates…an answer to my lifelong dream

When we confessed our love I experienced a euphoric change

The way you make me feel words haven't been created to explain

Love is the most powerful force on the face of the Earth

Because of your love I'm born again and had a rebirth

We all have flaws but when I look at you…perfection is what I see

My soul was dark and your love is the light that guided me

I've always wanted to ask…do you have to walk the way you do

I have to admit I get weak at the knees when I'm looking at you☺

Something mesmerizing happens when I look in those pretty brown eyes

They're so captivating I become awestruck and feel paralyzed

Look at the night sky and find the brightest star if you're feeling blue

Close your eyes and meet me at that star and I'll be there waiting for you

Thoughts of you make my heart race in a unique and special way

The sensational person you are makes me fall deeper in love everyday

Loves Journey

You have captivated my heart—you are a miracle to my soul
Feelings reborn that had decayed…the truth be told
I would describe you as a benevolent and kind-hearted empress
I'm constantly daydreaming of your kiss, cuddle, and caress
Always remember when we are apart—I want you to know it's true
Out there…somewhere in this Universe I am thinking of you
Love is the most powerful and dynamic force one will ever see
For those who have experienced it—no doubt they'd agree
When I sleep each night I am forevermore dreaming of your smile
I've discovered that in your presence that life is worth while
What I need to live is provided to me by Mother Earth—that's clear
But…Why I need to live has been given to me by you—my dear
Beautiful lady my intentions are not hidden…you will become my wife
Someone to have and to hold and share the rest of my life
Your love puts the fun in together and the sad in apart
The hope in tomorrow and the joy in my heart
Darling my love for you is a journey—starting at forever
It is my Alpha and Omega…therefore it ends at never

Afterthought

I am truly one of the good guys—a strong man with a bad boy edge

Treat women with tender love, admiration, and respect

A handsome, responsible and successful man…

I often ponder—think—reflected and sought

With all of these attributes why am I an Afterthought?

I know your favorite colors and do things "just because"

If it makes you happy, smile, bring you joy—you can count on me for sure

Massage your feet after a rough day in heels—run your bubble bath with

Scented candles and a glass of wine

Just relax beautiful lady your body, spirit and mind

You will always be treated like royalty—a majestic queen indeed

Have always had your back and support you each fight you've fought

I once again ask—with all of these attributes why am I an Afterthought

My partners tell me to become a dawg...bow wow!
A Rottweiler at that

Hit it and quit it that's what you need to do…

Don't get all wrapped up emotionally that shits not good for you

A woman doesn't know how to treat a good man—treat her like a bitch!

Fellas I can't go out like that—it's just not my style

A hopeless romantic that's defines me through and through

I hold women in high regard and view them with splendor to be loved and cherished

Listen up! No matter what has happened previously in the past

Regardless how many times my heart gets caught

I now have a woman who loves me and no longer treats me as an

AFTERTHOUGHT!

Broken Heart

Death by a thousand cuts the most painful torture known to man

There is another type of pain much more excruciating…I wish
I could ban

Pain of a broken heart…the misery…the hurt…the anguish
…the pain

My will and want to live has left…too much of an emotional drain

Can't focus…can't sleep…a headache…sick to my stomach
…no appetite

Depression so deep and dark…like a black hole absent of
energy and light

I lay in the bed wondering…contemplating what happened
and why

The only thing I felt like doing was curling up in a ball and cry

The pain is so agonizing the most unbearable hurt I've ever felt

I ask God what have I done to deserve the hand I've been dealt

All broken up on the inside the hurt is agonizing and
tearing me apart

It's said time heals all wounds…and is the cure for a broken heart

I can't go on…the end is here…turns out that heartbreak is
my demise

Death by broken heart…I'll call it a life and say my goodbyes

Hurt and Pain

The way I feel right now…maybe death is not a bad
option or choice

I want to scream and shout "I quit"…"I tap out"…at the top of
my voice

I'm all torn up on the inside…mortally wounded…I'm hurting
real bad

The way I feel is so much more devastating than sad

I'm not looking for pity or sympathy that's definitely not the case

I couldn't handle knowing that someone else has taken my place

My hopes and dreams shattered…my world as I know
it…destroyed

There is nothing or no one in the universe that could ever
fill your void

I can walk away knowing I gave it my all in this thing we call life

The decision is made…no more stress…no more crying
…no more strife

It is what it is…I fought hard…I fought the good fight

Nothing left to say or do but my final I love you and
final good night

Miss Chocolate

Smooth--decadent—sweet—luscious—addictive
A beautiful soft complexion of brown…but she's not predictive
Nestlé's—Hershey's—Whitman's—Godiva—Mars
She's a rare chocolate that can be found only among the stars
Lusciously rich and enticing to both the palate and the eye
More appealing and fascinating to look at than a moonlit sky
A delectable…scrumptious and mouthwatering treat
Add some whip cream on top and she's ready to eat☺
Fresh strawberries immersed in chocolate—a tasty treasure
My banana dipped in Miss Chocolate a sensual pleasure☺
More appetizing than any chocolate I've had the pleasure to eat
Sweeter than all the candy you get when you trick or treat
It's said that chocolate causes sexual arousal—fiction or fact?
All I know is thoughts of Miss Chocolate is my aphrodisiac
Yep! Miss Chocolate is delectable—mouth-watering—lusciously fine
The best thing about Miss Chocolate is that she's mine

Token

A tailor made Armani suit with Johnston & Murphy's on my feet
Fresh fade—manicured nails—looking sharp—looking sweet!
I not only have a college education—a Wharton grad at that
Articulate—well spoken—a super intelligent cat
Be assured when I open my mouth to speak
I am well prepared to apprise you of the info you seek
Not only do I dress the part—I know my craft—I've paid the price
Baffled—perplexed…why am I treated like the anti-Christ?
They say he has passion—my analysis…filled with emotion
No matter how exact they don't appreciate my devotion
Often amiss—you say he is creative and thinks out of the box
I provide conclusive facts—that's defined as conjecture
…or ad-hoc
When I speak…constant interruption…objections of every word
Okay I get it now...you want me to be seen and not heard
Looks good for marketing—diversity—my spirits not broken
I thought I'd made it but the reality is—you see me as a token

Never

I am not one to look at the world simply as black and white
I view the world as a cornucopia of hues…some dark…some light
Made up of different shapes…colors and sizes
Like a rainbow after the rain stops and the sun rises
While maintaining their individual unique style and look
Yet collectively a beautiful creation as ordained in the good book
As I go through life minute by minute and day by day
There is a conflict in what people actually do and what they say
Diversity—a concept—a theory corporate America say they embrace
We welcome people of color…religion…ethnicity and race
Let me tell you it's a joke…Wow! We made it…bro this is great
It's not diversity you fancy…we are expected to assimilate
You don't desire our input an affirmative head nod will do just fine
Dare not open your mouth…definitely don't speak your mind
I was called rebellious…unpatriotic…people had a lot of things to say
Because I choose to celebrate Juneteenth in lieu of Independence Day
On July 4th, 1776 the Declaration of Independence was signed
It provided freedom for some of our ancestors but definitely not mine

140+ years have past since Abe emancipated my folks
and set us free

It took 2+ years after that before all learned officially

This was before email so delivering the word took a little while

It took until June 19, 1865 to be delivered to Galveston Isle.

This is a topic rather not talked about…some would
like it dismissed

This is when we get angry… to be blunt downright pissed

You want to know when will we forget…when will
the debt be paid?

This deserves a proper response not one characterized as jade

The question is easy and not much of a challenge or endeavor

The answer is quite simple and not complex at all: **NEVER!**

I Discovered Something Today

No matter how educated...no matter our level of skill

Noted Harvard Professor Gates arrested! What the hell's the deal?

Six times more likely to be incarcerated than my brethren of white skin

They get probation...our ass get sent straight to the pen

I Discovered Something Today

Being treated like this aint just a trip it's a whole damn journey

We're a people of prominent Doctors—CEO's and Attorney's

This shit is damn wrong on so many different levels

Maybe Malcolm wasn't wrong when he called them devils

I Discovered Something Today

You say WOW! He sounds angry—not anger...I'm pissed off

Judged by the color of our skin—no matter how well Tiger plays golf

Thurgood Marshall won Brown –vs. Board of Education

The Landmark Supreme Court Case that ended segregation

I Discovered Something Today

In 1963 a King lead a march and told us about a Dream

A sea of humanity this nation has never seen

You ask what have I discovered—what have I been taught

The Dream is not over—the battle will continue to be hard fought

Oprah

She is an American treasure an icon to say the least
The way it would be said "around the way" is that she's a beast
The epitome of the American Dream…going from rags to riches
The embodiment of what one can do even if you're digging ditches
She was born into poverty way down in the "Sip"
Right on the Natchez Trace Parkway…now she's making a serious grip
She has gained a tremendous amount of notoriety—wealth and fame
Truly impressive a Black Woman who did it with her brain
I'm not knocking any athlete—singer or actor
She did it in a profession dominated by white men a huge factor
The years of hard work paid off in 1984 it was now her time…her day
She took the talk show world by storm and like Sinatra did it her way
Television—Movies—Magazines—Philanthropy just to name a few
At this rate…maybe one day she will be President to
Some people don't like Oprah but that's all right
Showed us no matter where you start don't quit the fight
Thank you Ms. Winfrey you've done yourself and your people proud
You've upon doors for us that once said do not enter no entrance allowed

I Apologize

Such a beautiful woman both inside and out
An answer to a lifetime of prayers without a doubt
You have always had my best interest at heart
More style and class than a Picasso or any work of art
Your love is genuine and without condition
You've made loving me your number one mission
Your tender, love and care has made me rich beyond imagination
You're the absolute best that exist in God's vast creation
Even when I'm trippin with anger and unjustified emotion
You're right by my side with tender love and devotion
I know better than to judge others that's not how I was taught
I ask for your forgiveness for my bad thought
I am ashamed of what I put you through you deserve the best
You would never hurt me...you're nothing like the rest
My love for you is higher than any mountain—totally off the chart
Forgive me—I'm sorry—I apologize from the bottom of my heart

Pursuit of Happiness

"Life, liberty, and the pursuit of happiness" the inalienable rights of man

Protecting these God-given rights soldiers have fought across many lands

I thought once I have money and the right job that will do the trick

Once I achieved this...happiness would come quick

I soon learned this enjoyment and exuberance lies within me

Bill Gates will tell you...happiness is not for sale it's absolutely free

Skeptics have asserted that happiness is just a state of mind

Don't listen to the cynics remember happiness is what you define

Happiness: Good fortune—joy—contentment—elation—pleasure

I have found that special someone who I absolutely treasure

Happiness brings me tranquility and that makes everything bright

She keeps my mood jubilant thus all in my world's a delight

What keeps my spirits high? What makes me look forward to the sunrise?

Awakening to another day in which I can look into her eyes

I'm elated when I bring her peace of mind and calm to her soul

Her happiness will always be my number one goal

No more searching for my soulmate...no further need to roam

My pursuit of happiness is complete...she's turned my house into a home

The Dream

I'm not afraid of heights…earthquakes or to fly on a plane

I don't have a fear of tornados…typhoons…or hurricanes

I fear that young African Americans will forget our history

It is vital they know from whence we came so it's no mystery

Thurgood Marshalls fight Brown v. Topeka Board of Education

At one time we weren't free to go to school were we wanted in this nation

Before Dr. King and others marched we didn't have one civil right!

In the past we couldn't vote because we weren't white

There was James Brown before Jay-Z…Little Richard before Lil Wayne

Pioneers…trailblazers who paved the way so we could entertain

Can you know where you going…if you don't know where you've been?

If not you are destined to repeat past failures and that would be a sin

Freedom is not free to get where we are our ancestors went through hell

Let us not forget the Dream is not dead…the Dream is alive and well

Final Destination

A person who lacks judgment or sense…idiotic person
…a weak mind

I thought I had found that lady…that one of a kind

I lead with my heart instead of my head… broke the number
one rule

That's why once again I sit here alone like a damn fool

I've said it before and I'm going to say it again

I want someone to love me for me is that a sin

She's my modern day queen…someone of royalty

Was I asking too much for someone to be loyal to me?

She is my everything…maybe I should give up and quit

Success is not worth a damn thing if you have no one to share it

I saw all the signs…they were right in front of my nose

It was as apparent as the petals of a blooming rose

Did I see it coming? Yep! It was as plain as day

I not only saw it but I heard that huge train coming my way

This time around…I gave it my all—mind—body and soul

Being treated badly and being shit on is sure getting old

This has caused so much internal combustion and commotion

Psychologically—mentally I don't know if I can handle
the emotion

I'm all broken hearted not knowing whether I want to live or die
This shits not supposed to happen…I'm a damn good guy!
What do I do next...What's my next move from here?
Well…maybe I should call it a lifetime and just disappear
I wonder if a person can die from a broken heart
Right now death is not a bad choice…I'm falling apart
I've had a good life…lots of good times and celebrations
But tonight I accept that I have reached my final destination

By Myself

I gazed upon the midnight horizon at a breath taking moon
It was a sweltering summer evening in the month of June
Yet another moment viewed by one when it was meant for two
Tears fell from my eyes—once again missing is you
Invariably I will be in love with you…eternally…till
the end of time
Seems so hard to spare a second for me…has no reason or rhyme
A case of the blues causing anguish, depression, and strife
Deep routed sadness never encountered in my life
I begin to bury my feelings, pull back and guard my emotion
Heartache—Troubled—Distraught…such internal commotion
Altogether too much hurt…entirely too much pain
Enough mental suffering I think I'm going insane
Once again waiting—sense of despair—my mood…dejected
You say everything's ok…yet I feel rejected
Love is a living thing and does not die easily—that's 100% correct
It thrives in the face of all life's hazards, except excuses and neglect

Confession of Love

Anyone can catch your eye…it takes someone special to catch your heart

You are that special someone who has captured my heart

Before your love I was just existing—just waiting to die

With your love I've discovered life is a natural high

I miss you so very much whenever we're apart

But I always feel warm inside because you're always in my heart

When I hold you in my arms it feels like time stands still

Elation—Jubilance—Euphoria best express how I feel

I cherish every moment we are together your presence is all I need

It motivates me to go on and inspires me to succeed

My heart jumps for joy whenever I see your beautiful smile

The manner how you carry yourself with elegance, grace and style

I love you so much…sometimes I begin to cry like a little boy

Not from sadness or heartache—I am overwhelmed with joy

We hold hands…I feel the aura of love exuding from your fingertips

Every passionate kiss the sensation of love is felt through your lips

Some people say you truly only fall in love once in your life

When I think of you, I fall in love with you all over again my future wife

Since you have been in my life—no moments of sadness or feeling blue

I exclaim to the world I am so very much in love with you

I hereby confess to you my true love—no if, buts, or depends

True love never has a happy ending because true love never ends!

Heart Ablaze

Who you've been with before…don't matter that's all in the past

Don't care who was first, second, or third I just want
to be your last

Feelings of deep passion and unbridled desire

Affection never felt before…my heart is ablaze—on fire!

A silhouette of beauty and loveliness…that I will always cherish

These emotions are heartfelt they'll last forever and never perish

Holding you tightly in my arms…such a divine and warm embrace

My own slice of paradise our exclusive private place

Walking hand in hand while gazing at the moonlit sky

Happiness so uncontrollable…I began to weep…I began to cry

I stared deeply into her eyes…at that very moment time stood still

Extraordinary elation—incomparable bliss—what a thrill

Angelic…Graceful…Delicate…Sexy…Yes! So damn fine!

Rarer than a precious jewel you're one of a kind

Woman of my dreams…everlasting destiny…certainly
worth the wait

My best friend—my lover—without question my soul mate

God has blessed me…without a doubt I know it's true

Effortlessly…I proclaim—I AM IN LOVE WITH YOU!

ILY

Did I tell you today…that I am deeply in love with you?
No other person or feeling in this world will ever do
I love you because you're not fake…you're a genuine girl
Your love…affection and kindness brings serenity and calm to my world
I love you so very much because you're wonderful…amazing….remarkable to name a few
All of these plus…from the top of your head to the bottom of your shoe
I love you because you're so very beautiful both inside and out
Your delicate touch makes my heart scream and shout
I love you because you have made my heart warm…whence it was cold
Your tender love and care has captivated my mind—body and soul
I love you because you are now and have always been my dream
You've made my hopes a reality and given me the peace of a stream
I love you for yesterday's memories...today's love and tomorrow's hope
Your thoughtfulness and understanding made it possible for me to cope
I love you not only for who you are, but for what you are making of me
A man intensely in love with you…more intense than the roughest sea
I love you because you saved my life and gave me a chance to start anew
Did I tell you today…that I am deeply in love with you?

Genuine Girl

Free from pretense—full of sincerity—a loving soul
without a doubt

The epitome of beauty both inside and out

She is more stunning and finer than the most exotic lace

Nothing! I mean nothing...can compare to her charm and grace

A vision of loveliness—lips ever so soft—smile so delicate
and bright

Allure of the rising sun and tranquility of a full
moon at night

Her exquisite smile...YES! That smile as subtle
as the morning dew

She breaths rarified air I am certain that is true

Rarer than a Picasso—more unique and vibrant than any stone

Definitely worth the wait...each and every moment alone

As kind and gentle as a summers breeze in July

An angelic and delicate voice that makes you say: My! My! My!

The personification of elegance—the embodiment of
a Nubian Queen

Without a doubt the greatest depiction of a woman ever seen

You ask: "of whom do you speak"...Who is this most
precious pearl?

The woman of a lifetime of dreams...she is my GENUINE GIRL!

I Need You

There is quite a significant difference between a want and a need

A want is a desire…not required…not a necessity
as some perceive

A need is necessary…something essential…as vital as breathing air

A need crucial for my well-being is your tender, love and care

Not ashamed to let the world know I need you to cope
with life's travels

If I am deprived of your love…my being…my psyche unravels

I need your soft touch…as delicate and fine as a grain of sand

You make me feel good all over…with a simple stroke
of your hand

When you professed your love…you gave me a priceless
gift of a lifetime

Yes! True love...no more valleys to cross or mountains to climb

My darling you are truly the embodiment of unconditional love

You're the blessed angel that my life has always been in need of

To live…my primary needs are shelter…air…food and water to

My heart is yours and in order to live most importantly I need you

Good-to-Great

The sun a helluva lot brighter—the stratosphere the most dynamic shade of blue

Normal has become extraordinary—my outlook on life totally new

Situations that once occurred in which I've cried

Now thoughts of her bring me joy…a warm…soothing sensation inside

Her vibrant beauty is second to none

The jubilance and bliss that rings out when she calls me HUN!

Her smile is breathtaking…her laugh illuminates a room

A brand of loveliness seen less often than a blue moon

Unique…different…. a novel idea that sets me apart

Think with my head—Nah! I'll think with my heart

My heart had grown cold—certainly had given up on love

Whew! It snuck up on me with the tranquility and peace of a dove

Is it possible…has it really happened to me?

I have assuredly met the woman of my prayers and dreams

At one point in my life I didn't believe in destiny or fate

Because of her…my life has now changed from good-to-great

Character

I was upfront and told you all the good…the bad…the right …the wrong

You said you would judge me for me...I finally felt like I belong

Words spoken from your mouth…I am your dream come true

You've never had anyone respect and treat you as good as I do

We are talking about the past…because of some external jabber and noise

Right now…I'm just trying to stay cool and maintain my poise

From the very beginning I told you about my illness …treatments and all

Now you have doubts about me…what nerve…what gall

How does one defend himself against something that may never occur?

Make an assessment of me based on what's happened that's what I prefer

I am the man who has been there for in your greatest time of need

I'm a person of great character and I've shown that in word and deed

My character has been honorable…I treat you with dignity and respect

If you need me I'm there and definitely not guilty of neglect

I told you once before…**Listen to your heart and not that outside chatter**

Hear who your heart says I am and that's all that really matters

I Wish You Were Here

I wish you were here so I'd be in the presence of dignity and class
A display of elegance never seen before...be it present or past
I wish you were here so I could smell the scent of your perfume
Aroma fresh and delicate as spring flowers in bloom
I wish you were here so I could see your alluring smile
Dynamic—luminous with lavish grace and style
I wish you were here so I could look deeply in your eyes
So honored you'll become my wife—the ultimate prize
I wish you were here to soothe my mind and spirit
Whispering sweetly into my ear so I can barely hear it
I wish you were here so I could caress and hold you tight
Giving me peace and tranquility throughout the night
I wish you were here so I could kiss your lips so soft and sweet
With such emotion and warmth...your heart skips a beat
I wish you were here so I could thank you for loving me
Unconditional love higher than any mountain and deeper than any sea
I wish you were here so I could passionately make love to you
Arousing sensations...yet gentle and sensitive as the morning dew

Lost For Words

I love you with every breath...every smile and every teardrop of
my lifetime

You are proof that a lifetime of hopes...prayers...and dreams
do come true

I have traveled all over and seen countless extraordinary and
beautiful people...places and things

You are the most stunning...loveliest and fascinating of them all

Love is an emotion a unique special feeling that can't
be defined in words

80,000 words in the dictionary...yet still not sufficient to explain
the deepness of the love I feel for you

I could live an infinite number of lifetimes and express to you my
love every second of each day

It would not be enough to illustrate the abundance of love I have
for you in the depths of my heart

A Moment

The love we have for each other is an exquisite—timeless moment

A moment so exceptional our worlds stop when we look
into each other's eyes

A moment so priceless the beat of our hearts are in symmetry…one
with the other

A moment so precious our emotions poor out and our hearts are
filled with joy

A moment that exceeds anything humanly imaginable we never
want it to end

A moment so incredible we gasp for air because the moment is so
breathtaking and rare

A moment so fascinating we are seduced by the power of our love
for each other

A moment so genuine…the realization that a lifetime of dreams
and aspirations had finally come true

A moment so amazing that each and every day with you is a
special and magnificent day

With you in my life everyday is a very special day…I hope you
know how much I cherish…

All of our moments together…and how much I treasure you

With All My Love!

Sign of the Times

We are the richest nation in the world…the entire universe

Can't even get a job at Mickey D's…makes you want
to scream and curse

Bankruptcies and foreclosures occurring pretty much everyday

The only thing left to do is get on our knees and pray

People have to choose between eating and putting gas in their car

We as a people have to do something before this goes too far

This issue is shared by all people and not based
on the color of your skin

Some folks can't afford their medication that's a shame and a sin

The fix can be found in the quote: "United We Stand Divided
We Fall"

Not individual self serving actions…it's going to take us all

Remember: The needs of the many outweigh the needs of one

Politicians of all parties need to get it together and get
something done

The common good a specific goal that is shared and
beneficial for all

We need to listen to each idea and suggestion no matter
how big or small

Listen up America this is a call to arms…time to pay attention
We have to pull together as one…no fighting or dissension
It's time to get started on that journey we have a huge hill to climb
I don't want to hear it's a sign of the times
What if Dr. King…Sister Theresa and JFK had that attitude?
None of that defeatist talk…I aint in the mood
Let's sit down and talk and put our plan together right
There's no time to fuss…argue…scream or fight
We will pull together and beat the economy and then take on crime
Truly a nation united…THIS will be our sign of the time

False Love

I have an emptiness inside that has been barren my entire life
Only one thing can fill that void and that's you as my wife
I have done every and anything that I know to do
From my perspective the rest is up to you
I don't know if you realize...I only see you a few times a week
I respect and understand your situation that's why I don't make a peep
Lord knows I have been patient and tolerant as we progress
However I have something important I must confess
I sit around the house waiting...hoping to see or hear from you
When it comes to spending time with me you have something to do
I've given a little here...I've given a lot there
From my point of view you have not given anywhere
One person always giving and the other one always taking
The relationship will be difficult and painstaking
I've thought about this long and hard and you've left me no recourse
I have no other choice but to file for divorce

Pay It Forward

Luke 12:48…To whom much is given…much is required

Not asking you to give away things you have worked for and acquired

The idea was the brainchild of Ben Franklin…he did more than fly a kite

He developed a way to help his fellow man out of his plight

The concept can be initiated by anyone at anytime in their life

Whether they are son…daughter…husband or wife

You do a favor for a person…but instead of repaying you

They must bless three others who are in need of help to

Imagine a world in which each person's primary goal is helping others

No more selfishness or greed…central focus on helping another

No more homeless…no unemployment…no one without healthcare

This would be the answer to all of our hopes and prayers

I know it won't be easy…but we'll never know if we don't try

So let's give it a shot…if it works our limit is the sky

Behind Every Good Man is a Phenomenal Woman

As far as I was concerned I did my best…I fought the good fight

I accomplished a lot…no longer viewed my future as promising or bright

I had a space that was barren and dead as a desert on the inside

My breath of life was gone…my emotions had shriveled up and died

Each day filled with sadness…Id lost my hearts melody and song

Like a summers day rain…out of nowhere you came along

A mind more brilliant than the finest sapphire…ruby or topaz

So attractive and a personality with so much fire and pizzazz

Your care and concern changed me like the colors of the leaves in fall

You gazed at me…your eyes sparkled like diamonds …I felt ten feet tall

Sensing my needs...we drew closer…our lips touched in pleasure divine

Kiss as powerful as a tornado in a volcano…chills up and down my spine

Most notably you focused on my mind as well as my heart

You made deposits of knowledge and wisdom…which
you did impart

You were vital…essential in rebuilding my confidence
…faith in myself

Awakened and inspired I moved forward and put
the past on the shelf

My inspiration…you taught me it's ok to fall nine times
…just get up ten

Phenomenal…you are…so I will pick myself up and try it again

Invisible

Once when you awoke the first thought on your mind
Dear Lord thank you for this wonderful man…he's one of a kind
Before God we vowed we would be with each other forever
Now we don't even go to bed together
As each day goes by it has become quite clear to me
I must have become invisible you see
You no longer greet me with a smile or hug
If anything your demeanor has become rather smug
My ideas or feelings are no longer valid they are soon dismissed
As the ramblings of an unstable man, who has no sense
As each day goes by it has become quite clear to me
I must have become invisible you see
You now look right through me as if I am not even there
Talking or spending time with me seems more than you can bear
You're never at home…I dare not ask where you've been
Based on your reaction one would think I committed a sin
As each day goes by it has become quite clear to me
I must have become invisible you see

Feelings

Love...is a strong affection, attraction, admiration, and devotion
Unrivaled passion, tenderness, fondness, and unequaled emotion
I discovered something that I could not ignore
Admittedly, I've never been in love before
I thought I had fallen in love in the past
But those feelings somehow…someway never seemed to last
Right now…today I apologize sincerely from the bottom of my heart
For those I said I loved and eventually we broke apart
At that moment, at that time, at that place
I honestly thought love had filled that empty space
Quite frankly I don't know because the emotions
That I am feeling I have never felt before
Please don't look bewildered or even perplexed
To care deeply for someone does not have to involve sex
"Yes"...I said it I can't believe it either!
When she wraps her arms around me to give me a warm hug and soft embrace
It always…always puts a smile on my face!

Choices

I find myself often wondering, what life has in store for me

Will I find someone special? Be alone…what's my destiny

God allows us to make our own choices whether they're right or wrong

I learned from my bad choices—made me smarter—made me strong

It's time to try something new…I'm going to get out of my own way

Yeah! That's what I'll do…I'll start right now—today

First…I am going to close my mouth and open my ears

Listen to what others have to say even if I shed some tears

I wasn't a good listener…I was more focused on what I had to say

I'm certain I ignored some words of wisdom being that way

Second…I will be less enamored with "I "and pay more attention to we

I will change—adjust—adopt a different philosophy

No more doing things for glory—admiration—praise

I will definitely change my attitude and my ways

Last…but certainly not least and truly as important as the other

Let her know how much she's loved and appreciated my brother

She is absolutely an extraordinary woman the likes I have never seen

I will focus on her wants—needs—desires and treat her like a queen

Soul Mate

Indeed I found my Soul Mate by first finding me
She rescued me from a life of unhappiness, depression and grief
She loves me for me with all my imperfections and flaws
My life has new meaning and you are the cause
I climbed the highest mountains and searched the oceans blue
I knew my Soul Mate was out there I just had to find you
Soul Mate love conquers haters, cynics, and ego
It's everlasting—like a flower…feed it and watch it grow
My universe is inspired by you—my heart needs to have you near
I look to the heavens and I'm so grateful and sincere
So many of my smiles and laughter depend on you
An answer to a lifetime of prayers—a dream come true
For richer or poorer in sickness and in health
I swear a vow of unconditional love to my last dying breath
Loving thoughts of you when I go to bed at night and
when I first awake
You're my hearts destiny—my love—my predetermined fate
My paradise—my heaven on earth—definitely worth the wait
The woman of my dreams and fantasies yes! My Soul Mate

Your Legacy

One's word and—or commitment that something will be done

Take it to the bank it's guaranteed... a person's word is their bond

You can count on me...I promise...I'll do it...Don't worry
I got your back

All phrases that have to do with promise and commitment
...not slack

Back in the day a handshake and a person's word was all you need

Today...a handshake...a person's word...can't trust it too
much greed

A big issue is selfishness and people only care about what's
in it for them

We all need to become more caring about the other or
our outlook is grim

If I tell you I'm going to do something I do it every
time without fail

When I ask you...I get excuses and a look that says go to hell

If you say you are going to be here at six don't show up
two hours late

Then cop an attitude when I ask why you didn't show up
until eight

After all is said and done our character and words will be
left behind

Will your legacy be considered selfish or one who helped mankind

Unconditional Love

We concurred this is a good move and it would benefit me and you
More quality time with each other that is well overdue
The time we spend together has not increased it's been a lot less
I don't get it...why has the time we spend together started to digress?
I find myself looking at the phone...hoping...praying that you call
The sound of your voice will do...another 24 gone and nothing at all
I no longer get excited when you say you're coming over to chill
I've heard it all before...an excuse and another promise unfulfilled
I've learned to hold back my enthusiasm and my emotions I subdue
Don't get me wrong there is no one I prefer spending time with than you
Deeply in love we know it with our look...our touch...our feel
Often left shaking my head wondering what's going on ...what's the deal?
Something's on your mind...the look in your eyes...the tone of your voice
Lay your cards on the table...you talk...I'll listen...this is the wise choice
My love is unconditional...I am committed to us for...forever and a day
I'll be by your side...no matter what you've done or have to say
I'm your lover and best friend...bare your soul...nothing additional
I won't judge or criticize...my love is everlasting and unconditional

Vows

Solemn promise—pledge—personal commitment—heartfelt declaration
I hereby pledge unconditional love to you…my life's sensation
I promise to provide and take care of all your needs
For this is my covenant—my oath—my creed
I will be your rock…for you to lean on in times of despair
Providing you with comfort—tender—love and care
I vow to love you for richer or for poorer in sickness and in health
Having you for a wife is worth more than all the worlds' wealth
I commit to you my eternal love and a lifetime of marital bliss
When we go to sleep each night it'll be with a hug and a kiss
Beautiful lady I vow to love you each and every day more…
Affectionately—passionately than I loved you the day before
I vow to keep a smile on your face and a melody in your heart
I will do this with undying love from the very start
I'll protect you and ensure nothing harms a hair on your head
I would give my life for you—enough said!
I pledge to you my life as a loving and faithful mate
I am 100% absolutely certain this is our destiny…our fate

Language of Love

Romance is the language of love…there are many ways to say
I love you

It's not the size of the prize it's the little things you do

A car needs gas…a baby needs food…your relationship
needs romance

These are the things you need to do to give love a chance

Show your love with not only your words but your actions

A love note…mail her a card…give her a hug and watch
her reactions

No one ever gets tired of being loved…I promise

You can take that to the bank…don't be a doubting Thomas

Tell her you love and appreciate her if you can't think of
anything to say

Take her out on a date like you use to back in the day

When you leave for the day and come home at night…seal
it with a kiss

Consistently do this each and every day and I can assure you
a life of bliss

Don't ignore the importance that affection and intimacy has
on the soul

No matter your age you are never too old

Be spontaneous…impromptu…and don't forget to have fun

Having your lady as your best friend is second to none

Whether you take her on a date…walk on the beach
…or out to dance

You now know the language of love is romance

My Biggest Fan

Is there for me in good times and in bad
Whether I'm pissed off or extremely sad
In my time of trouble and time of need
When I needed a shoulder to lean on...yes indeed
Rather I'd scratched my knee...or fall down and go boom
Excruciating pain from a broken heart or need someone to talk to
When your friends have turned their back on you
You can count on this person to be loyal and true
Wouldn't let anyone talk you down or cause you any harm
To them you will always be "Hun"—their little charm
Kick you in the ass when needed...also there when you needed a hug
Would tell you—"you're a child of mine and I didn't raise no thug"
Always has a way of making things all right
No matter what time of day or night
If I needed a counselor, guardian angel, or a real friend
This person was there in the beginning and will be there in the end
You wonder...Who is this saintly person? Better than any other
This person is my biggest fan of all, this persons MY MOTHER!

The Gift

It is a wonderful thing when you bring joy to the lives of others
Rather it be your mom…dad…sisters or brothers
My darling it's not magic…you have been anointed with a special gift
Mere mention or thought of your name…My spirits do lift
This gift that has been bestowed on you is the rarest of all
It can't be found online…in the store or even a shopping mall
Your gift is a priceless one in which a value cannot be placed
When you're around…my anxiety and worries are instantly erased
My world is definitely a better place because of you
So tranquil and peaceful…joy abounds and my days are never blue
When you are around calmness and serenity permeates throughout
You have been touched by an angel without a doubt
I now have residence in my own piece of paradise
Thanks to you my world is so lovely…so extremely nice
You have been granted a unique gift infrequently seen
One that brings good cheer to others…that's few and far between
The inner strength you have…the finesse to silence any tiff
You've indeed been blessed by God with such an amazing gift

Little Princess

A blessed remembrance of times past and the joyous occasions of the now
The anticipation and the promise of the forthcoming
High energy—effervescent…an adorable and beautiful child
She has an infectious laugh and a Hollywood smile
Elation to her mother's heart and the apple of her eye
Truly a gift from heaven blessed by God upon high
A handful sometimes…a heart full of joy all the time
A little angel full of innocence…one-of-a-kind
She has the ability to illuminate your day and warm your heart
An extraordinary God given gift which sets her apart
A divine blessing a little girl with zeal and spunk
Perfect medicine after a hard day to get you out of a funk
You can feel the spirit in her soul—see the adventure in her eyes
A priceless jewel a mothers dream…the ultimate prize
A number of things in this world bring us delight and pleasure
Nothing equals our angelic little princess to love and treasure

Dear Mom

I don't know where to begin…I don't know where to start
I have so much to say about you…from my soul and my heart
You have always been there for me…in good times and in bad
You're there for me whether I am angry…depressed or sad
Whether I needed a counselor, guardian angel, or just a friend
You have shown me that you'll be there through thick and thin
When all others had forsaken and turned their backs on me
You would be my shoulder to cry on and give me serenity
Sometimes you gave me tough love…back then I didn't understand
Now that I'm a woman…I know why you had to stick to your plan
I was blessed because for a role model I didn't have to look very far
All I had to do was look right in front and me and there you are
There is something so very special about a mother—daughter bond
You taught me so much and have provided for me above and beyond
Mommy…I love you and you are better than any other
I would like to thank you so very much for being my mother

Deception

I don't exactly know what's going on…but I know something aint right

You need to come clean…because what's done in the dark will come to the light

Oh what a tangled web we weave when first we intend to deceive

You lying to me hurt and you know it's my pet peeve

A statement made with intent to deceive or convey a false impression

Now that you've lied…everything you say I have begun to question

Love is truly blind…I was warned…now I wish I had heeded their advice

Think you can say the moon is made of cheese and I'll ask you for a slice

It pains me to know you've been deceitful and deceptive

You won't go far in life because some people are quite perceptive

Fool me once shame on you…fool me twice shame on me

I have been as good to you as anyone could ever be

I gave you all my trust…my love and my undying devotion

You decided to stomp on my heart and play with my emotions

I hoped I was wrong and it was a false perception

But the reality is I got caught in your evil web of deception

My Reality

The planet Earth is as round as a circle most people believe
What is your reality from day-to-day what puts you at ease?
Tell me…do you see the world as round—triangle—square?
More importantly what do you do in your moments of despair?
Some people laugh…some scream...some even cry
Some look upwards to the heavens and simply ask…why?
What is your reality? What makes your world go
round and round?
Who or what is it that fires you up even when you're down
All of us need something to help get us through the tough days
You know…when life's circumstances leave us in a haze
I've searched all over…here and there…near and far
The place to look isn't here on earth but among the stars
I discovered something about my reality…it's not new or unique
My problem…I forgot the answer and instead walked in defeat
"The Lord is my light and salvation; whom shall I fear"
That is my reality…so obvious and extremely clear
Jesus Christ is our savior who loves us unconditionally
So you see my friends that is why he's My Reality

Special

I have a dream that one day I will be special to someone
A person who thinks of me with each rising of the sun
A woman who loves me just as much as I love her
Is it too much to ask for this type of affection to occur
I want to be loved and appreciated it's my primary desire and need
I would like to be special to someone in not only word but deed
I haven't asked the world for very much at all
I guess it doesn't matter because I'm always the one to fall
Just one time I want to be thought of first and not last
Think of me in the present tense and not the past
Is it selfish to ask for someone to be attentive to me?
I'm not asking for all of their attention just a small degree
I will do whatever it takes to keep her spirits high
I'll always do for her before myself and that's no lie
I haven't been greedy because I don't ask a lot for myself
All I ever wanted was to be special to someone else
Don't wait until the people you love…tomorrow has been taken away
Remember to appreciate your beloved and treat them special each day

Sunshine

It has been said that love is the poetry of the senses
Love is so powerful it can bring peace and mend fences
I would proudly like to announce that I am happily in love
Before I knew it…it swooped down on me like rain above
Because of you my heart now has a place to call home
I believe in love again…no longer a need to roam
If love is a gamble then being with you is a royal flush
What I feel for you…is unconditional love not some school boy crush
You are a rare and unique combination of elegance…style…grace
Thoughts of you always put a smile on my face
When I count my blessings I count you an infinite number of times
Is she a ten? Nope…she's a quarter not a dime ☺
Like the Earth to sunshine...my world revolves around you
Your love—affection and loveliness makes me feel brand new
Like sunshine on a cloudy and rainy day…you brighten my soul
Ensuring you're the happiest woman in the world…my primary goal
You give me inner warmth and have charisma that is one-of-a-kind
Now you understand why you are my sunshine

Time

Please…can we spend some time together?
Regardless of what you think we don't have forever
Time to hug—time to love—time to kiss
Time to look at the moon and stars and just reminisce
Time is more valuable than any diamond or gem
It's the one thing you can't ever make up to her or him
Time to appreciate—time to work—time to pray
No matter how rich, we all get the same amount of time each day
So please…spend your time more wisely than you spend your cash
Don't be careless and throw it away like yesterdays trash
Use your time doing things that your heart and soul desire
Don't let others control your time or your outlook will always be dire
I implore you...devote more time to those you love and who love you
It's the most beneficial investment of time that one can do
I leave you one thing to ponder: What is the one wish of a dying man?
A mansion—a yacht or a maybe a brand new Mercedes sedan
I think we all agree wishing those things would be a crime
That's right you guessed it they want more TIME!

Trust

The reliance in the integrity of…A belief in something as true
I can have faith in your word because what you say you will do
A wise person once told me: "Be cautious and careful it's a must"
Ensure you are judicious before you decide who to trust
Always remember: Trust is hard to earn but much easier to lose
It is certainly more valuable than any diamond or jewels
Many will say they have your best interest at heart
When their actual purpose is to tear you apart
Some bear false witness…while others will scandalize your name
Believe it or not they do it with no guilt or shame
Remember…people will abandon you when times get rough
But you know **"The One"** who'll be their when things get tough
No matter the circumstances or what you do
Put your faith in **"The One"** who'll see you through
When deciding who to trust please be extremely smart
Read Proverbs 3:5 and "Trust in the Lord with All your heart…"

Missing You

Does absence really make the heart grow fonder?

When I first heard this…not much thought nothing to ponder

I have a new found respect…I am now a believer that it's 100% true

Because…In my case I'm downright pitiful when I'm apart from you

I miss your presence and the sound of your angelic voice

I miss it because it makes my heart and soul rejoice

I miss your sense of humor and magnetic allure

I miss you because your love is genuine and pure

I miss your smile…your kiss and your warm embrace

I miss you softly stroking my back in that magic place☺

Most of all I miss you because of what you stand for and who you are

The love of my life and my shining star

Essence of Love

I am a man who understands your past and what
you've been through

I believe in your future...more importantly I believe in you

I was magnetically drawn to you like an eagle to the sky

Once in bondage my heart and soul was freed an you're
the reason why

I was starved for affection and had waves of passion inside of me

Deep down rooted passion that only your love could set free

Love is a condition in which your happiness is essential to mine

When I see your Kool Aid smile I know all is fine

Our hearts gravitated towards each other like the Earth to the Sun

Such a heartfelt and fervent belief we are meant to be one

I'd give you any and everything you ever wanted
as far as the eye can see

I could live infinite years and it won't come near what
you've given me

By no means am I a man of wealth but some say I'm pretty smart

I can only give you one thing and that's everything in my heart

Impersonal Truth

We said we would be honest with each other no matter
what time of day

Instead you dropped a bomb on me and then sped away

When I read what you said admittedly I was
stunned and perplexed

One we had talked about it before and two you sent a text

I've long gotten over what you had to say because it is the truth

What hurt is your method of delivery was impersonal and uncouth

Yes...it is a sensitive subject I know this to be the case

But issues like this needs to be discussed face-to-face

Technology is a great thing when used in the correct way

But not when you have something so delicate to say

This is history and in the past…I have one thing to say additional

I love you with all my heart and soul and my love is unconditional

Special Lady

We started out as friends…two people who would just sit and chat
Neither one of us had thoughts of anything more than that
As time went on I knew I wanted to be more than just a friend
I had to be careful…it was important that what we had didn't end
I had to take the risk…she was astonishing…I had to take that chance
The most amazing woman I have known you can see that at a glance
Finally got the courage to ask…oh my God...She said yes
She caught me totally off guard…I must confess
Having her in my life has exceeded my wildest dreams and imagination
My life has gone from dull and dead to my heart and souls sensation
I have fortunately been blessed with God's most beautiful creation

Remember When

Remember when…our eyes met for the very first time
I thought to myself such a beautiful woman…it should be a crime
Remember when…we had our first kiss
Such an amazing sensation of jubilance and bliss
Remember when…we exchanged our vows becoming unison of one
Our lives as husband and wife had just begun
Remember when…we spent time together
Be it rain—sleet or sunshine no matter the weather
Remember when…I could make you smile
Spending time with me was worth your while
Remember when…I was your first choice
Now I just wait and long for the sound of your voice
Remember when…I could call you anytime
Now you get upset with me for no reason or rhyme
Remember when…we looked forward to being as one each day
Now I just sit and cry hoping the pain will go away
Right now I just long for days gone by
When we laughed and smiled so much…but now I just **CRY!**

Beautiful Thing

I find myself dreaming of the day of our marriage
You and I riding together in a horse drawn carriage
The concept of marriage is such a beautiful thing
A man and woman joined forever by a kiss and a ring
For you are the woman God gave me to spend my life
My soul mate who is honored to become my wife
I'm looking forward to the day we become a union of one
I will then be your husband when you call me "HUN"☺
Radiant—magnificent...so wonderful my heart beams
An incredible woman to share my hopes and dreams
Priceless—invaluable worth more than all the gold in the world
Nothing fake or phony about her she's my Genuine Girl
As I look intensely—deeply into her eyes...what do I see?
An amazing woman who's completely in love with me
It's been said that the "Eyes are the window to the soul"
When I gaze into her baby browns I'm mesmerized—truth be told
Such an alluring woman...the most captivating I've ever seen
On bended knee...thank you Lord for my Lovely Queen

Fool in Love

The Spinners sang…"it takes a fool to learn that love don't
love no one"

I'm a fool because my love for you is more intense than
the blazing sun

Your smile is as brilliant as a rainbow after a spring rain

Dazzling eyes that sparkle as stars on a lake of champagne

Your beauty is so breathtaking…like a red rose in full bloom

An astonishing mind-blowing kiss as we stood under the moon

I am aware that love is a journey…you'll get no debate from me

But…I'll be taking this trip first class with the love of my life Gigi

Alone

When we first met nothing in this world could keep us apart
We were always hand-in-hand—side-by-side—heart to heart
Little by little…she wanted her distance…she needed her space
It was obvious to me she wanted me out of her face
Before you know it her love began to fade
Her attitude towards me was matter of fact and rather jade
Now when I hear her voice it has a different tone
Next thing you know I am all alone
How I long for her affection—kiss or a simple hug
I'm looking for any indication that I am still loved
Love is an action word a word of depth—passion—desire
One of strong emotion that keeps your heart on fire
Being alone is extremely solemn—somber—sad
A fate or destiny I wish on no man be he good or bad
I pray this night…Heart of mine please stay strong
Because once again tonight I am all alone

Enough Said

Just when I thought things are at its worst and I am in dire straits
The Almighty shows up not a moment too late
He hasn't abandoned me even when I've given up hope
He continues to pick me up…dusts me off so that I can cope
Why does he love me so much? Why does he even care?
Just as he promised…he is always there
In spite of all the bad and wrong things I have done
He still loves me unconditionally like a father loves a son
If not…he would have given up on me a long time ago
I don't understand why he hasn't…only he must know
He sees things within yours truly that I can't imagine or see
He must definitely have a purpose on Earth for me
I don't know what to say or do that has not been said or done
The obvious thing is to lean on the ultimate one
I am going to become what God has ordained yours truly to be
It took forty plus years to realize it's not about me
It's been easy to say but difficult to get it through my hard head
Jesus Christ is the answer…enough said!

In Too Deep

I'm one of the good guys…well at least I thought
I treat women with dignity and respect the way I was taught
If I'm one of the good guys and so damn nice
Then why in the hell does she treat me like the anti-Christ
Yes…I love her from the time I wake till the time I go to sleep
I know I can do bad all by myself…but I'm in too deep
When things are good they're very good…the best times I've ever had
Then the next minute she flips and treats me just as bad
She comes to visit me sometimes ten…fifteen minutes at most
Then I don't hear from her for hours…she disappears like a ghost
She says she's in love with me and wants to be my wife
Honestly…I don't know if I can deal with this the rest of my life
For a relationship to thrive one must be trusting and make that leap
Some say just leave her…it's not that simple…I'm in too deep
I've heard it so many times before…nice guys finish last
I am and will continue to be nice…in the future …present and past
I proudly proclaim to be a nice guy…a good dude and not a creep
I'm going to tough it out…I'm addicted and I know I'm in too deep

Understand

Understand I am here for you whenever and however you need me
Understand that my love is unconditional for eternity
Understand each and every night I thank God for you up above
Understand when I look into your eyes I see into the eyes of love
Understand true love is knowing your faults and loving you even more
Understand my heart skips a beat whenever you walk through the door
Understand I hate to see you go but love to watch you leave
Understand that when you're sad so am I and I also grieve
Understand that I'll do anything to bring joy to the recesses of your heart
Understand that I am so very sad when we are not together but apart
Understand my world revolves around you from sun up to sun down
Understand you are my Nubian Queen with a golden crown
Understand because of you my life is phenomenal—downright great
Understand you're my best friend—my lover—my soul mate
Understand my life is not measured by the breaths I take everyday
Understand each moment spent with you takes my breath away
Understand you are the reason I look forward to each day of my life
Understand I can't wait to the day you become my wife

I Believe

It's important for me to know that you believe in us
The foundation of a successful relationship is built on trust
From the moment we kissed...I knew you would become my wife
I believe and trust in you with everything...including my life
You are my soulmate I believe this with all my heart
There is nothing in this universe that could tear us apart
When I first awake I want to hear the gentle sound of your voice
I could have infinite options I would always make that choice
I believe in miracles...take a look at the woman in which I've been blessed
I can picture her laughing saying: "Boy...You're a Mess"
I absolutely know and believe you saved my life
Until I was blessed with you I was lost and destined to misery and strife
I believe you are the most beautiful woman this world has ever known
I've been graced with a majestic Queen to sit with me on the throne
Beyond a shadow of a doubt...I believe in you and me
I emphatically believe we were meant to be
I believe in our unison and that we will always be together
I believe our unconditional love for each other will last forever

Dream Girl

In the mirror I saw the wisdom and pain so old and deep
on my face

Reflection of a lonely man who never found anyone special
as I ran life's race

As the sands of time slowly flow through the hour glass

Have I missed my chance for love…have I let it pass?

I know I must open my heart to have a chance at love

So afraid of getting hurt…I pray for strength from above

You're the answer to a million sleepless and lonely nights

You're all I've dreamed of…you make my heart so
sunny and bright

My modern day miracle the woman of my hopes—dream—desire

You are my soul mate and you've set my heart ablaze on fire

I searched from one end of the earth to the other end it seems

The journey was well worth it because it lead me to you
the girl of my dreams

Rhetoric of Love

When I'm around you everything in my world is just right

Sound of your voice smile on your face make the most dismal days bright

Whether dark clouds—gray skies—any type of inclement weather

In my heart the sun is shining any time we're together

Your existence in my life gives me reason to sing and rejoice

Declaring my love for you at the top of my voice

It's like being touched by an angel so delicate and pure

I am in the presence of greatness that I know for sure

The style and grace of your walk is poetry in motion

So elegant when you enter a room it causes a commotion

You are your mother's little princess—will always be my queen

The finest most ravishing woman my eyes have ever seen

You have made all my dreams and fantasies a reality

Rejuvenated my spirit and increased my vitality

Sometimes I'm overwhelmed by your beauty—not knowing what to say

"I love you more today than I did yesterday and I will love you more tomorrow than I do today"

Gigi's Groove

I shed a tear tonight…not a tear of sorrow, or pain—a tear of joy
The sound of her voice, the presence of her smile
Has made my view of the world a lot more worthwhile
"Yeah I shed a tear tonight…."
It has been said that the eyes are the window to the soul
What is it that I see when I look into her eyes?
A beautiful woman…yes! An intellectual equal--without a doubt
But even more than that…a special and unique person
Someone equally as beautiful both inside and out…
"Yeah I shed a tear tonight…"
When I am around her I can't help but stare
At the most beautiful woman here or anywhere
Without a doubt one of a kind—the way she talks, walks, and smiles
Yeah, that smile…that makes time stand still and my heart skip a beat
"Yeah I shed a tear tonight…"
She probably doesn't realize it but she saved my life
No, not the physical life of pain, hurt, and strife…
My mental, psychological, and emotional being
I have actually found a modern day queen
A true lady—a woman of style and grace
No matter the time she always puts a smile on my face
"Yeah I shed a tear tonight…"

Someone

I have lied—manipulated—cheated and deceived
Therefore…I deserved all the bad things that I've received
You note the use of the word "have" indicating past tense
So to dwell or live in history makes absolutely no sense
Before I find that special someone…looking near and far as I can see
Thank God…I discovered I must first believe in me
Because of the Lord's grace I have another chance
An opportunity to get my life together…even a shot at romance
I've searched for someone who truly believes in me
That special and unique someone who's vital to my destiny
Someone who respects—trusts and believes in me and my decisions
Someone who believes in my dreams—ideas and visions
Someone I can trust each and every word they say
Someone who knows I will defend their honor without delay
Someone who does not despair at the first sign of trouble or strife
Someone I will spend loving completely the rest of my life

Home

A place where one should find harmony—peace and tranquility
Definitely not fighting—disputes and instability
The delectable fragrance of your wife's perfume
As you awaken from sleep in your bedroom
A sensational aura in which to wake by the one's you love
As you warmly look skyward thanking the Lord above
Thank you God for such a magnificent and wonderful life
He has rewarded my obedience with children and a wife
One encounter's very few priceless moments and events
If you're fortunate most will be shared with those heaven sent
Our humble home is our piece of heaven and paradise
The love that resonates… no other descriptive would suffice
We've been blessed with a loving—caring family and all of this
Therefore, we've dubbed it our kingdom of marital bliss
Home is where the heart is…this is definitely true
Our house is now a home because it includes me and you

Who I Am

What do you feel in your heart when you envision me?
Sadness and despair or exuberance, joyfulness and glee
How do you feel when I enter your thoughts and mind?
Another dude running game or truly a great man who is one of a kind
When you see me come into the room how do you feel?
Indifferent and apathetic or full of enthusiasm and zeal
Tell me…do my words match my deeds and actions?
Would you describe me as cocky or do I deliver satisfaction?
Who I am is a man that will make your hopes and dreams come true
That's my life's mission because I am in love with you
Who I am is a man who loves you with every ounce of his being
And I don't give a damn that the whole word's seeing
Who I am is a man whose entire world revolves around you
My happiest day on earth…when we exchange vows and say I do
You don't need to answer me or anyone else
The answer to who I am lies within yourself
Listen to your heart and not all that outside chatter
Hear who your heart says I am and that's all that really matters

Survive

A heritage of strong people who endure and know how to survive
We don't just make it by the skin of our teeth…we thrive
Survived slavery, Jim Crow and two Busch's in the White House
Can't treat us like shit and think we're going to be quiet as a mouse
If it's a fight that you want then it's a fight you'll get
You can't play us like Charmin and think we'll clean up your shit
You think we are dumb and you are so damn slick
Then you smile in our face…make me want to hit you with a brick☹
Not going to do that because that's what you expect or something worse
Not going fuss—fight—get angry—no profanity—won't curse
Do like Ali and the Williams' sisters and beat you at your own game
Nope we're not going to use violence…we're going to use our brain

I Asked...

I asked for entertainment...God gave me fun
I asked for light...God gave me the sun
I asked for food...God gave me grain
I asked for water...God gave me rain
I asked for a place to sit...God gave me a throne
I asked for a melody...God gave me song
I asked for a place to bathe...God gave me a brook
I asked for guidance...God gave me "The Good Book"
I asked for protection for my feet...God gave me shoes
I asked for happiness...God gave me you

My Love For You...

My love for you…is like a diamond…unbreakable and strong
My love for you…is entrenched in my heart right where it belongs
My love for you…is more powerful than any potion
My love for you…is deeper than the largest ocean
My love for you…is infinite and will last forever
My love for you…is everlasting and ends at never
My love for you…is extraordinary and not traditional
My love for you…is now and always unconditional
My love for you…is real and my passion is over-the-top
My love for you…is like breathing and I have no reason to stop

OOMPH!

I didn't believe in this thing called love…l-o-v-e

Those untapped emotions of joy, happiness, peace, and tranquility

I heard people talk and sing about this fascinating thing

One minute it was as calm as the wind blowing in the sky

The next as violent as a volcano erupting on a mountain on high

Why in the hell would I want to allow someone into this private place?????

One that could cause such a wide range of emotions unintentionally displaced

Have my heart ripped out and lose my mind no thanks

Each time someone gets close to that private place

I would say b-a-c-k u-p off me no entrance allowed

One day I met this girl just as beautiful and innocent as anyone in the world

I took a look a real quick glance and thought "what the hell" give it a chance

Her beauty was overwhelming; her smile was so bright,

My heart skipped a beat and I whispered to myself—man she is tight

She had this certain **OOMPH** that I had never seen

Yeah that certain **OOMPH**.....you know the indescribable sensation one feels

When you are in the presence of someone special and unique

She was definitely one of a kind so beautiful and sleek

At that very moment time stood still my eyes met hers and hers met mine

I knew then I was in the presence of the most powerful force in the universe

Yeah that's right...a woman with that **OOMPH!!!!**

Dear Love

Dear Love...some say you're a living thing...others say an emotion

I've heard you defined as affection...sweetheart...flame
...and devotion

Love...you are by far the universes most powerful force
known to man

I must say you have aged well...you've been around
since time began

I thought I knew you...I recently discovered I didn't know
you at all

Turns out what I truly knew about you was rather
limited and small

I thought you were based on what I did for people—easy enough

It's not what or how much...it's why I did it you cherish
...not the stuff

Admittance is free...you are unconditional...you apply
equally to us all

It doesn't matter whether I'm sick...healthy...poor...rich
...short or tall

I have made commitments and promises in your name in the past

Now that I have more wisdom of who you are I know
why it didn't last

You are as vital as the air I breathe… food I eat and water I drink

Radiant…clearer…tranquil…you have changed my view
and how I think

You're far too dear to lose…you're the inspiration and
the why I live

Love…I have someone special in my life and I now have
you to give

To find you I had to concede once I did a miracle ensued
out of the blue

Gigi came into my life and at long last…I have someone
to share with you

www.ingramcontent.com/pod-product-compliance
Ingram Content Group UK Ltd.
Pitfield, Milton Keynes, MK11 3LW, UK
UKHW041933190726
13854UKWH00004B/1567